A Note to Parents

DK READERS is a compelling program for beginning readers, designed in conjunction with leading literacy experts, including Dr. Linda Gambrell, Professor of Education at Clemson University. Dr. Gambrell has served as President of the National Reading Conference and the College Reading Association, and has recently been elected to serve as President of the International Reading Association.

Beautiful illustrations and superb full-color photographs combine with engaging, easy-to-read stories to offer a fresh approach to each subject in the series. Each DK READER is guaranteed to capture a child's interest while developing his or her reading skills, general knowledge, and love of reading.

The five levels of DK READERS are aimed at different reading abilities, enabling you to choose the books that are exactly right for your child:

Pre-level 1: Learning to read
Level 1: Beginning to read
Level 2: Beginning to read alone
Level 3: Reading alone
Level 4: Proficient readers

The "normal" age at which a child begins to read can be anywhere from three to eight years old. Adult participation through the lower levels is very helpful for providing encouragement, discussing storylines, and sounding out unfamiliar words.

No matter which level you select, you can be sure that you are helping your child learn to read, then read to learn!

DK

LONDON, NEW YORK, MUNICH,
MELBOURNE, AND DELHI

Series Editor Deborah Lock
U.S. Editor John Searcy
Managing Art Editor Rachael Foster
Art Editor Gemma Fletcher
DTP Designer Emma Hansen-Knarhoi
Production Georgina Hayworth
Picture Researcher Rob Nunn
Jacket Designer Simon Oon

Reading Consultant
Linda Gambrell, Ph.D.

First American Edition, 2007
07 08 09 10 11 10 9 8 7 6 5 4 3 2
Published in the United States by DK Publishing
375 Hudson Street, New York, New York 10014

Published in Great Britain by Dorling Kindersley Limited

DK book are available at special discounts when purchased in bulk
for sales promotions, premiums, fund-raising, or educational use.
For details, contact:
DK Publishing Special Markets
375 Hudson Street
New York, New York 10014
SpecialSales@dk.com

A catalog record for this book is available
from the Library of Congress

ISBN: 978-0-7566-2532-0 (Paperback)
ISBN: 978-0-7566-2533-7 (Hardcover)

Color reproduction by Colourscan, Singapore
Printed and bound in the U.S.A. by Lake Book Manufacturing, Inc.

The publisher would like to thank the following for their kind permission
to reproduce their photographs:
(Key: a=above; b=below/bottom; c=center; l=left; r=right; t=top)
Alamy Images: David Noble Photography 30b; Roger Hutchings 26t; Ron
Niebrugge 21; Pacific Press Service 4tl; Stock Connection Distribution 20bl;
Corbis: Rick Gomez 4b; Pete Leonard/zefa 25; James Noble 23t; Robert Harding
World Imagery 24; **Getty Images:** DK Stock/Christina Kennedy 5t; Iconica/Frans
Lemmens 13; The Image Bank/Peter Adams 19; Photonica/Doug Plummer 23;
naturepl.com: Aflo 17; **PunchStock:** Digital Vision 4cla; Medioimages 28;
Photodisc Red 12; Stockbyte Platinum 5br; **Science & Society Picture Library:**
National Railway Museum 25t; **Science Photo Library:** Martin Bond 11; Robert
Brook 27; Ted Kinsman 2b, 9t; NASA 31b; US Geological Survey 31cr; Tom Van
Sant, Geosphere Project/Planetary Visions 30; **SeaPics.com:** Doc White 15;
Still Pictures: T. BALABAADKAN/UNEP 20br; Randy Brandon 26b; ullstein -
Mehrl 21t
Jacket images: Front: **Science Photo Library:** Dr. Fred Espenak c; Tony
Mcconnell (b/g)

All other images © Dorling Kindersley
For more information see: www.dkimages.com

Discover more at
www.dk.com

DK READERS

Water Everywhere

Written by Jill Atkins

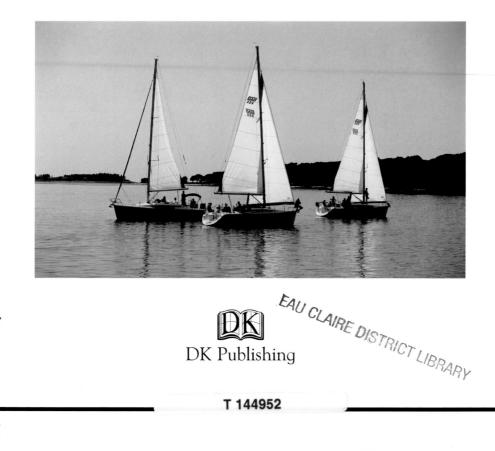

DK
DK Publishing

We use lots of water
every day.
We take baths
and brush our teeth.

We water the yard.
We wash our dishes,
our clothes, and
our cars.

We go swimming
and play water sports.

Washing hands

We wash our hands before meals so we don't get germs on our food that can make us sick.

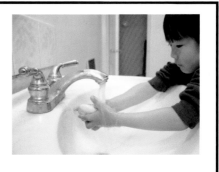

We also need water. We have to drink water every day to keep our bodies healthy and alert.

Water is the best thing to drink between meals.

Almost three-quarters of
the planet Earth is covered
in water.
Most of the water is contained
in five large oceans and several
small seas.

Mediterranean Sea

*Caribbean
Sea*

Sargasso Sea

*ATLANTIC
OCEAN*

*PACIFIC
OCEAN*

We cannot drink this water,
because it is too salty.
It would make us sick to drink it.
So how does this water become
the water we use and need?

ARCTIC OCEAN

Bering Sea

Arabian
Sea

INDIAN
OCEAN

Coral
Sea

SOUTHERN OCEAN

Tasman Sea

Water in the oceans and seas
is warmed by the sun.
The heated water becomes
droplets that rise up and
form clouds.
The wind blows the clouds
over the land.
Then the water cools and falls
from the clouds as rain.
Rainwater is called freshwater
because it is no longer salty.
Some rainwater runs
into rivers, which
flow into lakes or
back into the sea.

Snowflakes

In cold weather, water from clouds falls as sleet, hail, or snow. Each snowflake has a different pattern with six points.

This process is called the water cycle.

Our water comes from lakes
or natural springs under the ground.
It is cleaned so it is fit to drink.
Underground pipes carry the water
into our homes.

Storing water

Sometimes a dam is built across a river to make a reservoir. Some of the water we use is stored there.

It is important that we do not waste water. Adults can help save water by fixing leaky pipes. You can help by remembering to turn off faucets.

Animals also need water
for drinking and bathing.
Elephants can suck more than
two gallons (7.5 liters) of water
into their long trunks.
They squirt this water
into their mouths to drink
or over their backs to keep cool.

The Arabian, or dromedary, camel is nicknamed "ship of the desert."

Camels can store water
in their bodies.
They can live more than five days
in the desert without a drink.

Many creatures live in the ocean and cannot survive without water around them.

Some hunt or hide in deep water where it is cool and dark.

Others swim near the surface, searching for other animals to eat.

Gills

Fish have gills on the sides of their head so they can breathe underwater. They can't live out of water.

Plankton

Some whales, such as
the blue whale, eat millions
of tiny creatures called plankton.
These whales have long comblike
bristles instead of teeth.

Fish that live in rivers and lakes are called freshwater fish.
Many freshwater fish eat plants that grow in the water.
But some big fish, such as pike, eat small fish.

Many birds and animals live near
water, where they find their food.
They eat water plants, fish,
insects, or other animals.

Plants need water to grow.
Their roots push down
under the soil to find water.
They take in water
through their roots.

A cactus can grow
in the dry desert
because it stores
water for
a long time.

Rice is grown in countries
where there is a lot of rain.
This is because rice can only grow
in flooded fields.

In many places,
there is so much rain
that it causes floods.
People's homes are washed away.
In other places, there is sometimes
hardly any rain at all.
This is called drought.

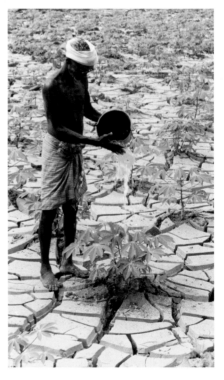

Sometimes water becomes
a dangerous power.
For example, strong currents
in the sea can wash people away.
The most powerful form of water
is a tsunami, a giant wave.

Water looks different when
it gets very cold or hot.

Liquid   *Solid*   *Gas*

The water we drink is liquid.
As water becomes very cold,
it freezes.
It becomes solid ice like
the frozen seas at the North Pole.
As water gets very hot, it becomes
steam and vanishes as a gas.

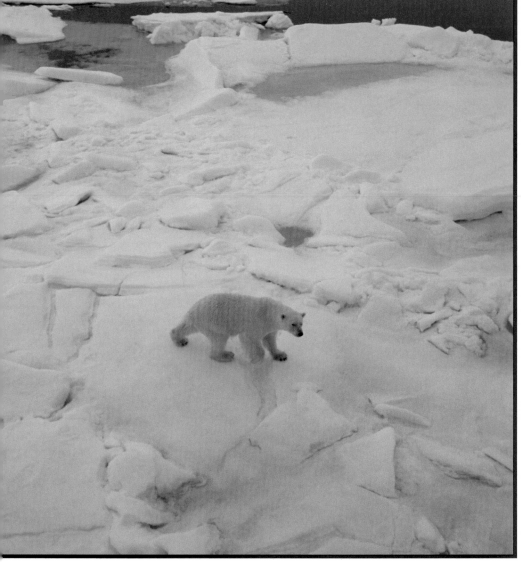

Steam

The steam from boiling teapots or steaming saucepans is dangerously hot and can burn you.

Water can be used to move
and power man-made machines.
The wheels and cogs of
a water mill are turned by water.
Rushing water is sometimes used
to make electricity.

The Rocket

One of the earliest steam-powered trains was the Rocket. George Stephenson invented it in 1829.

Steam has been used
to power machines
for more than 250 years.
In a steam engine,
water is heated
in a large tank
to make steam.
The steam is used
to make the engine go.

It's important to keep
the world's water clean.
If a ship carrying oil crashes into
rocks, oil pours out into the sea
and harms the wildlife.

*Bird coated
in oil*

If a factory allows poisonous waste
to escape into a river,
this pollutes the water.
It can kill all the life in the river.

If children drink or play
in dirty water, they can catch
very dangerous diseases

Many objects are absorbent.
This means that water
soaks into them.
If we go out in the rain,
our clothes absorb the water
and we feel wet.
Towels also absorb water
so they help us get dry.

Many objects, such as umbrellas, are non-absorbent, so water does not soak into them.
They are especially useful for keeping off the rain!

Water is very important
to every living thing.
Without it no humans, or
animals, or plants could exist
on this planet.

Scientists and astronauts
have been exploring other planets
for signs of water.
If they find water, it might mean
that life exists or used to exist
out there in space.

*NASA's Mars
Exploration
Rover*

Water Facts

Did you know that there is water in most things, including us? Our bodies are more than half water. Jellyfish are almost all water.

The longest river in the world is the Nile in Africa.

The deepest part of the Pacific Ocean is the Mariana Trench. There is no deeper place in any ocean.

The Caspian Sea is really a lake, since there is land all around it. It is the biggest lake in the world.

Two-thirds of the water used in a home is used in the bathroom.

Today, at least 400 million people live in areas where there is not enough freshwater.